Triumphant;
Created For Victory
~
Destined For Glory

~Marnie Baker~

I see you riding on horseback. You are riding in complete freedom Freedom! You will carry the mantle of Freedom. You will NEVER stop riding that Freedom Horse. Freedom Marnie

Copyright © 2016 by Marnie Baker
Published by Asher Yields Publishing
Library of Congress Catalogue Card Number
ISBN- eBook - ISBN: 978-0-9972974-0-9
ISBN- print - ISBN: 978-0-9972974-1-6

All rights reserved. No part of this publication may be reproduced, distributed, or transmitted in any form or by any means, including photocopying, recording, or other electronic or mechanical methods, without the prior written permission of the publisher, except in the case of brief quotations embodied in critical reviews and certain other noncommercial uses permitted by copyright law. For permission requests, write to the publisher, addressed "Attention: Permissions Coordinator," at the address below.

Asher Yields Publishing
8206 Rockville Road
Box 268
Indianapolis, In 46214

Edited by: Lawrence Wole {a missionary evangelist serving God's Will, with ministry base in Africa} & Marnie Baker

Cover Design by Avanadesign: More of her work can be found at: https://uk.fiverr.com/avanadesign/design-a-stunning-professional-book-cover

Lettering illustrations by Jordan Jennings; Pens and Needles Co. More of her work can be found at pensandneedlesco.etsy.com and on Instagram at @pensandneedlesco

(https://www.instagram.com/pensandneedlesco)
Email - pensandneedlesco@gmail.com

"Scripture quotations taken from the Amplified® Bible,

Copyright © 2015 by The Lockman Foundation
Used by permission." (www.Lockman.org)

The Living Bible copyright © 1971 by Tyndale House Foundation. Used by permission of Tyndale House Publishers Inc., Carol Stream, Illinois 60188. All rights reserved. The Living Bible, TLB, and The Living Bible logo are registered trademarks of Tyndale House Publishers.

THE HOLY BIBLE, NEW INTERNATIONAL VERSION®, NIV® Copyright © 1973, 1978, 1984, 2011 by Biblica, Inc.® Used by permission. All rights reserved worldwide.

The ESV® Bible (The Holy Bible, English Standard Version®) copyright © 2001 by Crossway, a publishing ministry of Good News Publishers. ESV® Text Edition: 2011. The ESV® text has been reproduced in cooperation with and by permission of Good News Publishers. Unauthorized reproduction of this publication is prohibited. All rights reserved.

"Scripture taken from *The Message*. Copyright © 1993, 1994, 1995, 1996, 2000, 200, 2002. Used by permission of NavPress Publishing Group."

Scripture quotations marked (NLT) are taken from the Holy Bible, New Living Translation, copyright © 1996, 2004, 2007 by Tyndale House Foundation. Used by permission of Tyndale House Publishers, Inc., Carol Stream, Illinois 60188. All rights reserved

Scripture taken from the New King James Version®. Copyright © 1982 by Thomas Nelson. Used by permission. All rights reserved.

Dedicated to God;
my Heavenly Father,
my LORD, and my King.
For without Him there is no me.

~Marnie~

Acknowledgments

If you have ever held my hand, given me a hug, or have said to me *"I love you"*- to you I, humbly and sincerely, say *"Thank you"*. I extend to you the highest of honor, for you have helped to shape and inspire me into becoming the person that I am today. You are a part of the story of my life, you have been included in the plans that God has for me, and I thank each of you from the bottom of my heart. I love you!

~Marnie~

Table of Contents

Introduction	viii
Chapter 1: God Outside My Box	1
Chapter 2: Like No Other	4
Chapter 3: Broken Glass	8
Chapter 4: Hopeful, Hope-filled, Hope	13
Chapter 5: All Is Well	16
Chapter 6: But God	19
Chapter 7: Overcomer	23
Chapter 8: Communing With You	27
Chapter 9: Freedom	31
Chapter 10: Triumphant	35
Part 1: The End, and The Beginning	35
Part 2: Zion	41
Part 3: Our Wellspring	44
Part 4: The Dawning	45
Part 5: An Anointed Army	46
Part 6: Fulfillment Achieved	48
Part 7: Time Without End	50
Chapter 11: Stronger	53
Chapter 12: Mindful	56
Chapter 13: Peace Is What I Need	59
Chapter 14: They Thought They Had Me	63
Chapter 15: Am I Doing My Very Best	66
Chapter 16: With Him	71
Chapter 17: New Clothes	74
Chapter 18: Better, Stronger, Faster, Greater	77
Chapter 19: My Commander	81
Chapter 20: Comforter	85
Chapter 21: I Am His	87
Chapter 22: Mine	90

Chapter 23: Up   93
Chapter 24: Good, Better, Best   96
Chapter 25: I Am Home   98
Chapter 26: Redeemed   103
Chapter 27: Warriors Goal   106
Chapter 28: I Need Him   109
Chapter 29: Our Day   112
Chapter 30: Gaining Everything   116
Chapter 31: There's Always A Choice   121
Afterword: Salvation Prayer- Personal Message   126

Introduction

Hello my Triumphant friends,

Triumphant; Created For Victory ~ Destined For Glory is my first published book and I am very excited about the plans that God has for it.

When God first placed the idea for this book within my spirit, He gave me a clear vision of what He wanted to express through each of the story poems. That vision was *'Triumphant'*.

As a result, I knew the key message of what He wanted to share with each person who would be reading these pages. That message is that in life we will go through tests and trials; we will be hurt, we will grieve, and we will endure. These tests may leave us feeling tired, beat up, and empty. In other words, there will be times when difficult trials may knock us down and make us want to give up and quit.

At those times it is critical that we do not remain down, and that we do not quit. Of course, getting up or staying in the battle can, at times, be difficult. Nevertheless, we should always recognize and remember that we are not people who should remain down or quit. There is a vital key that we must grab on to which helps us to get up when we are knocked down, and which helps us to revive when we have quit. That key is Jesus Christ.

We are joint heirs of Christ, and with Jesus' victorious Resurrection we have inherited a Triumphant life through Him. Triumphant is what we are, and it is forever instilled inside each of us. Triumphant is the territory that we are created to live our lives in. Triumphant is the weapon that we carry every single day and within every situation. Yes, difficult challenges may knock us down, but we are not people who remain down. We are a people who are forever able to live Triumphantly in absolutely every way and within all things that concern us. Do you realize this about yourself? Do you know who and what you truly you are? You are Triumphant! You must know who you truly are in order to be all that you are meant to be.

How many of us eat, sleep, and breathe the fact that we are Triumphant? Why is it that we do we not walk through tests and trials resting in the fact that that we are Triumphant in every way? With Jesus, we have everything that is Good and Perfect on our side and working on our behalf. Furthermore, we have an Excellent, Almighty God sitting upon a Mighty and Powerful Throne; a Throne of Love, care, and tenderness for each one of us.

Triumphant; Created For Victory ~ Destined For Glory was written to partner with the Holy Spirit to help bring the Truth of being Triumphant to your spirits.

This world needs God; not everyone is doing well, and countless people are hurting. You will notice that the words and the story poems in this book reflect this fact. The beautiful part about all of this is that God sent an Amazing Answer to all of our problems; His Son Jesus. One of the missions of Jesus' earthly ministry was one of Love, mercy and grace; He came for the sick and the broken hearted. Jesus is our Problem Solver, and He meets us where we are and at our needs.

My prayer is that this book does what it was written to do; allow the Holy Spirit to minister to people who are in need of God.

God loves you. His Love for you is not a Love which just happens to include you. You are not simply lumped into the enormous body of His children and Loved by default. No, God's Love for you is a Love that is intimately and profoundly meant specifically for you.

No matter what we are going through, and no matter how trying our situations may be, our faith in God yields restoration and deliverance. Jesus, and everything about Him, brings forth real hope and true victory. He is The Promise gifted to us by The Father, and He is the Firm Foundation on which our faith and trust are anchored upon.

This awesome truth, along with the exquisite and intimate Love that God has for each of us, has hugely influenced my decision to write professionally.

I wrote this book for all hearts; for the Christ follower, and also for anyone who is searching for and seeking answers about the amazing and overwhelming Love of God.

God is the only Living and True HOPE that the world has. He is The Answer that you are looking for. There is no other answer. Everything else is a falsehood or a counterfeit.

God's Love is so Pure and so Perfect that it is incapable of failing or falling short. God is always for us and never is He against us. He has the very best plans at the center of His Being for you, and for me.

In the midst of the challenges that we face- when we do not see or feel God within our situations- is when our faith and experiences with Him should rise above the pain, the worry, and the fear.

God knows what we are going through and is there with us, through it all. We should remind ourselves that feeling or hearing Him is not a requirement for Him to be working diligently and purposefully on our behalf.

I wrote *Triumphant: Created For Victory ~ Destined For Glory* for each one of us. It was written so that we have a poetic and lovely reminder that-although we each have our personal journeys to walk-we have a Friend, a Hope, and a Loving God Who believes that we are precious and worthy.

Let us hold fast to the fact that, come what may, as long as we have The Great I AM we have EVERYTHING we need to live Triumphantly in Jesus Christ. Therefore, at all times, we can boldly and confidently say *"All is well."*

Rest in His Abundant and Wondrous Love my friends,

*Now thanks be to God who always leads us
in triumph in Christ,
and through us diffuses the fragrance of
His knowledge in every place.*
2 Corinthians 2:14, NKJV

Triumphant

trī-ˈəm(p)-fənt

Definition:

Having achieved victory or success;

~

Experiencing or displaying triumph

victorious, successful, dominant, conquering, undefeated,
jubilant, exultant, elated, rejoicing,
joyful, joyous, delighted,
gleeful

Definitions by;

Random House Kernerman Webster's College Dictionary, © 2010 K
Dictionaries Ltd. Copyright 2005, 1997, 1991 by Random House, Inc. All
rights reserved. **Collins English Dictionary – Complete and Unabridged**
(http://www.thefreedictionary.com/_/misc/HarperCollinsProducts.aspx?
English) © HarperCollins Publishers 1991, 1994, 1998, 2000, 2003

Now come,
join me
on a journey
of learning where our
True TREASURE
lies,
and of embracing and experiencing
being Triumphant
in Jesus Christ.

~Marnie~

Majesty

*Mightier
than the thunders of many waters,
mightier
than the waves of the sea,
the LORD
on high is mighty!*

Psalm 93:4, ESV

We know that God is Creator and Ruler of all existence everywhere, and of the things that are known and unknown to us. We recognize His Omnipotence, His Omniscience, and His Omnipresence. We acknowledge that He is God alone and capable of doing the impossible. We know that He is Love Itself, and that He is Perfect and Pure in every way.

However, there are times when we contain God in an invisible box of our limited beliefs, thoughts, and imaginations. We readily admit that we know certain great and wonderful things about Him, yet there are times when we unknowingly put limits on an Infinite, Limitless, and Almighty God. I wrote *God Outside My Box*, to ask and answer the question - *"What if we allowed God to be God?"*

God Outside My Box

What could and would happen
    if I fully set God free?
Removed Him from the box
    unknowingly placed there by me?

What if I allowed God
    to spread His Powerful Wings?
Taking me to great heights,
    seeing new and amazing things?

Unknowingly, my thoughts and words
    "He can't"…"Too big"…"Not possible",
boxed my faith, curbed my hopes, hindering
    the full Truth of His Gospel.

MARNIE BAKER

What if I truly took Him
    at His Righteous and Holy Word?
Words so pure; the very *Best*
    my spirit has ever heard.

What if believing the impossible
    I certainly and faithfully did?
That fears, doubts, and worries
    were not my wavering minds lid?

The answer is so simple,
    so lovely, and is *KEY*;
He could create, fulfill, restore -
    move mountains just for me.

I would hear Him very clearly,
    following closely as He led.
His Comforting Rod and Staff beside me,
    by His Spirit I'd be fed.

My heart would be set free
    to soar, so high- be cleansed.
No longer seeing my life, my dreams
    through a dark and narrow lens.

His Words, His Life, His Promises,
    I would sincerely treat as pearls.
Together we would move and shake
    this country, this nation, this world.

What if I let God be God
    and removed Him from my box?

Treasured

*And the very hairs of your head
are all numbered.
So do not worry!
You are more valuable to him
than many sparrows.*

Matthew 10:30-31, TLB

Having your identity sourced from, and rooted in, God is critical to your spiritual journey here on earth. Knowing the truth of who you are to Him, and accepting how and what He feels for you, gives you your wings. The revelation that you are truly and deeply *Loved* by God allows you to soar to heights unimaginable, and to scale the highest of mountain tops.

Being secure in your identity in His Love helps to soothe all pains, helps to heal all wounds, and gives you a freedom that is limitless. This priceless treasure comes from knowing that your Father in Heaven truly, deeply, and unconditionally *Loves YOU* without limit or measure.

~Marnie~

Like No Other

To God you are like no other,
 to Him you are His choice.
You, yes you, the one He formed
 with His Will and with His Voice.

His Breath, His Spirit, His Greatness
 you carry deep inside.
His Love, His Heart, His Desire for you
 is where you should abide.

To God you are like no other,
 to Him you are His friend.
He yearns to give, to see you through,

TRIUMPHANT

to reside so deep within.

His Heart's Desire, His Love so true,
    He gave it all for you, yes you.

A Tremendous Love; a Terrific Love,
    a Love that does Its *BEST*.
A Love beyond compare and doubt,
    Extraordinary - above the rest.

Own it surely; what's yours is yours,
    and never let it go.
It is unique for all in Heaven above,
    and for each of us below.

To God you are like no other,
    you are cherished through and through.
Wonder, joy, and peace are yours
    when His Love inhabits true.

Grab it and take it; run with it,
    and own it as your own.
Love with it, lead with it, live with it
    for it comes straight from His Throne.

For to leave it lay and never know
    the true depth of who you are;
your value, your worth, your priceless self -
    His eyes-They see no scars.

To God you are like no other,
    this Love for you is so.
A Love that's free - and without strings,
    PRAISE God! You do not owe.

To God you are like no other,
    separate from all the rest.

MARNIE BAKER

Accept, receive, believe; no doubts,
you are simply His very best.

To God, you are like no other!

Cherished

For we are God's masterpiece.
He has created us anew
in Christ Jesus,
so we can do the good things
he planned for us long ago.

Ephesians 2:10, NLT

There are times when our trials require us to radically believe that God will do for us what we think is the impossible. It is then that it may look and feel as if we are being asked to climb a spiritual faith mountain; a mountain that has treacherous and uncharted pathways - of which every step is covered in shards of broken glass. To some, this path may seem scary and enormous; such are the spiritual mountains that God may ask us to climb. I wrote *Broken Glass* during a time when my spiritual mountain felt this way. At that time, God was asking me to believe that He would do, *just for me*, what I thought was impossible.

I had a decision to make, and I did. I decided that God was *trustworthy*. Also, I deliberately chose to believe in Who and What He is. Furthermore, I activated radical faith in my Faithful Father; the One Who Loves me the most. After that decision was made I was *'all in'* with God, come what may. Therefore, after walking a painful and treacherous faith journey, I reached the top of my mountain *Triumphantly* with Him.

It was then that I was able to look back and see that I needed my mountain to be exactly as it was; with all of its tears and laughter, and yes, shards of broken glass. For who I had become was a better, stronger, and more powerful me in God than who I was when I first began my faith climb.

Broken Glass

A pathway covered in broken glass
is the mountain I'm asked to climb.
My trust unclear, so deep my fears,

TRIUMPHANT

my faith *MUST* act.
It's time.

When asked to believe, to hope, to dream
what's required of me is deep.
It takes much more than what I have,
so drained, so tired…I weep.

To believe that God will move for me
while I walk on broken glass;
to trust Him no matter what I see,
so steep that mountain pass.

To believe that my life God will heal,
to see past pain and fear.
Rely on His report, and His alone
seems so far; not quite so near.

Bring peace to my mind, my life, He will
of this I must believe.
Despair and torment I do forsake,
His Hope I shall receive.

To believe the impossible - I must hold true
for the sea indeed to part.
This is to walk on broken glass
says my fears, and not my heart.

My heart needs what is found in God,
it demands of Him and cleaves.
My faith and trust must be so strong;
No doubts.
I must believe!

He grieves to see me hurt so deep,
tears pouring from my eyes.

MARNIE BAKER

My doubts - He wants to set me free
of this I can't deny.

He feels my pain and knows my fears,
my worries, my lack, my doubts.
Yet, by my side, and through it all
He remains throughout the drought.

In this season, within each step,
I learn of Him for sure.
No matter how bad it truly is
with God I am secure.

Without Him I could not survive
the tests, the trials, the hurt.
For He is my Rock, my Sword, and Shield
and remains always alert.

Alert to my thoughts, my wants, and needs,
my desires, my hopes, and dreams.
For God is the Rock of my Salvation;
the One who Reigns Supreme.

I choose Him and leave the doubts behind,
for no hope is found in pain.
With God all things are possible,
this **Truth** I shall proclaim.

Life, Peace, Hope, and Victory in Him
they are forever found.
I shall rest underneath His Sovereign Wings,
and there I'm no longer bound.

It's hard at times to remain at peace
when life can bring you down.
But God, and truly God alone,

TRIUMPHANT

can see me towards my crown.

For He is not a far off God;
He is close to me and knows
that darkness seeks to overwhelm,
to bring me down so low.

To destroy my life, my hope, my joy;
to forever keep me bound.
Yet, God is *LIGHT*, and *LOVE*, and *STRENGTH*
Ever-present, and all around.

Hope to my trial sweet King do breathe,
peace to my heart please bring.
Your Glorious Presence around me,
Your Hand I shall always cling.

The path does look like broken glass,
it feels like hell on earth.
Yet, God is God - with none beside
bringing each a brand new birth.

Rest in Him, and trust in Him,
and never let Him go.
For Jesus is King; is Lord and Life-
in Heaven, and on earth below.

Triumphant

God is my strength and power,
And
He makes my way perfect.

2 Samuel 22:33, NKJV

TRIUMPHANT

God is Hope which delivers Heaven directly to your heart. Having your hope sourced from God is like having all of the possibilities of the universe available to you. The wants, needs, and desires of your heart are no longer impossible; for with God *ALL* things are possible. Blessings come when God is your God because He brings to your life an abundance of vibrant and dynamic *hope.* Thank You LORD for being the True Hope of the world.

Hopeful, Hope-filled, Hope

A living spring inside of me,
so lovely, so blessed - a necessity
and filled with endless possibilities;

Hopeful, Hope-filled, Hope.

Where shall it take me?
Soaring; so far, and so high.

What shall I see?
Faith; so deep, and so wide.

Shall I see my mountains crushed before me?
Will I no longer have to cry?

Shall I see the laughter twinkling
in my baby's love filled eyes?

MARNIE BAKER

Shall I see my body healed and whole;
healthy, strong, and true?

Shall I see my loved one saved and sealed;
refreshed, redeemed, renewed?

Shall I hold my true love's precious hand,
and forever beside them will I stand?

Hopeful, Hope-filled, Hope shouts *YES*,
and propels me from above.

The nourishing, sustaining, resounding spring
comes from God; Who is our Love.

And when at last that day is here,
when *HOPE-FULFILLED* arrives.

I shall dance amongst the glittering stars
in a velvet, timeless sky.

J

~Dedicated to Angel~

Everlasting Love

*Know therefore that the
LORD
your God is God,
the faithful God
who keeps
covenant and steadfast love
with those who love him
and keep his commandments,
to a thousand generations*

Deuteronomy 7:9, ESV

MARNIE BAKER

I wrote *All Is Well* on a day when I thought that I should be feeling and doing better than I was. Sometimes we beat ourselves up because we believe that we are not acting powerfully enough, being brave enough, or walking in the peace that we should. This poem addresses those difficult days and times. It also shares that no matter what we are going through - be it at the beginning, throughout, and at the end of it all - there is, and always shall be JESUS!

~Marnie~

All Is Well

I crumbled today.

My circumstances hit me hard;
like a freight train crashing into my chest,
robbing me of my peace.

Tears fell from my eyes when I crumbled today.
The axe of brutal reality aimed, swung,
and fractured me with its heavy, iron blade;
shattering all of my trust.

My knees buckled - as tears fell from my eyes-
when I crumbled today.
Something evil, sharp, and cruel came along
and viciously cut the muscles that held
together my hope.

My spine gave way - after my knees buckled -

TRIUMPHANT

as tears fell from my eyes - when I crumbled today.
A lightning bolt of disbelief struck and bent me in half;
disintegrating my faith - like ash.

My head struck the ground - because my spine
gave way - after my knees buckled - as tears fell
from my eyes - when I crumbled today.
Fear so terrifying crippled my thoughts;
silencing my joy and laughter.

My heart tried to fail
when my head struck the ground
because my spine gave way
after my knees buckled
as tears fell from my eyes
when I crumbled today.

But Jesus said
"No. I shall not allow this heart to fail!"

And grasping it tenderly in His Hands,
He holds it in Love,
smiles at me,
and says

"I AM HERE, and ALL IS WELL!"

hopeful

Fear not, for I am with you.
Do not be dismayed.
I am your God.
I will strengthen you; I will help you;
I will uphold you
with my victorious right hand.
I am holding you by your right hand-
I, the Lord your God-
and I say to you,
Don't be afraid;
I am here to help you.

Isaiah 41:10, 13, TLB

TRIUMPHANT

How wonderful it is to have a Living, Loving God who profoundly cares for you, and for me. Therefore, because He Is *LOVE*, and because He Is Care, there is a Hope that is Real, True, and Able which is there for us. With God, we can walk through any situation with a hope that is everlasting because He is alive, well, and sitting *Forevermore* upon His Mighty Throne.

But God...

Despair like vulture wings continuously
beat at my heart.

How do I keep the walls
from crumbling down all around me?

Do you see me my Lord; My God, My King?
I stand here struggling trying my best to hold up
four crumbling walls with only two small hands.

I'm hopeless. I'm helpless.
I'm desolate. I'm pained.
I'm alone.

But God...
Means that Hope Lives.

But God...
Means that Help arrives.

MARNIE BAKER

But God...
Means that Love, on Comforting Wings,
comes for me-comes to see me through.

But God...
Means that an intentional Love surrounds me,
is here for me.

With Jesus by my side, how magnificent, beautiful,
and sustaining is the phrase *But God...*

And for that reason My Help is the Word;
The Word which is God.

God is my Hope. God is my Light.
God is my Strength. God is my Shelter.
God is my Love, and He is always at my side.

So, I will rest in Him because He is my Strong Tower.
I will place my hope in Him because He is my Source,
my Strength.

I will put my faith in Him because He is Worthy and True.
I will forever Love Him because He is my Everything.

My situation does not make Him less God, because
He is there for me- Strong and Mighty.
Therefore, I am able to lie in His Comforting Arms
and rest when I need to.

Yes, I may walk through the valley of death,
yet, I will not fear the terrors because He Lives,
and He is with me.

Therefore, what was meant to harm me must now bow
down before Him to be turned around for my good.

TRIUMPHANT

Thank You Lord that there is a **But God** for my story, for my soul, and for my life.

Redeemed

*"I have told you these things,
so that in me you may have peace.
In this world you will have trouble.
But take heart!
I have overcome the world."*

John 16:33, NIV

Early one morning, as I walked past my front door, the tree in my yard caught my eye and *Overcomer* landed in my spirit. Life will present us with many challenges that we must walk through, yet God is always there with us during our times of trouble. However, we are not always rescued from having to walk through trouble as Shadrach, Meshach, and Abednego being thrown into the fiery furnace obviously proves.

Nevertheless, these incredible men beautifully demonstrated that no matter what their outcome was going to be that it was God who was the God of their lives. God made His Presence visibly known to all who were around while they were in the *midst* of their fire. So yes, things will happen; trials will come and storms will arise. God never promised any of us that we would not have trouble. His promise was that He will be there with us in the midst of our difficulties. As long as you have God as the God of your life you have everything that you will ever need to faithfully walk through every challenge.

<u>Overcomer</u>

From your tree
    some leaves will fall;
    browning your thoughts,
    and muffling your call.

From your sky
    some rain will drop;
    drenching and drowning,
    so powerful…you stop.

MARNIE BAKER

From your heart
    Some tears will shed;
    pain and grief
    its friend instead.

Along your path
    Some rocks will land;
    sharp and jagged -
    gashing your hand.

If breath remains
    and your heart does beat,
    you shall labor and trial;
    be sifted as wheat.

Yet, God is still God,
    He loves us so dear.
    For He cares and He treasures,
    He wraps us so near.

Your mind must know Him
    when some leaves do fall,
    and browning thoughts
    try to silence your call.

Your life must be His
    when some rain does drop.
    For He protects and shields you
    from making that stop.

Your heart He must rule
    when tears it does shed.
    For He Who is Peace
    shall be its Friend instead.

Your path He must own
    when rocks they do land.

TRIUMPHANT

He makes them smooth-the path straight-
holding tightly your hand.

When it falls, when it drops,
when it sheds and lands
the time to choose
is now at hand.

Yes cry, yes scream,
yes grieve, and weep.
Yet, always remember
that God is your Keep.

He is Mighty and Strong,
Loving and True.
Within the depths of His Being
is a shelter for you.

Built for you to rest,
to be nourished - forever embraced.
So be at peace, filled with Love,
and enjoy life's great race.

praise

When I said, "My foot is slipping,"
your unfailing love,
LORD,
supported me.
When anxiety was great within me,
your consolation
brought me joy.

Psalm 94:18-19, NIV

TRIUMPHANT

I am blessed to have a relationship with God that sustains me in every possible way. My heart is from Him, my life is from Him, and my future is from Him. God is The Greatest, and The Most Wonderful Love of my life. I nurture and treasure our relationship and our times together. *Communing with You* was an early morning experience that He and I had together that I wanted to share with you.

Communing With You

Early morning sunlight streaming through my windows,
urging me awake; brushing sleeping remnants from my mind.

I am awake and You are here;
Loving me, and smiling down upon me.

I am instantly hit with Your *LOVE*.
I am more alive than I have ever been before.
For You are here…with me.

You have watched over me through the night, haven't You?
As always, You watched over me as I slept.

Staying so close that I could feel You pressing in near me.
Keeping me in perfect Peace.

You are always so near me.
Tendrils of Your Extraordinary Love are continuously

MARNIE BAKER

caressing my mind, my heart, and my life.

I am awash in Your Glory and Your Loveliness.
So Abounding, so Wonderful, so Magnificent You are.

Your Presence in the room fills my spirit.
We communicate without words;
they are not necessary between us now.
Love and Joy pours from You.
I grab unto them like a starving soul;
embracing them within myself, holding on for dear life.

You are Life. You are my life.
I smile. I am blessed. I am so thankful.
I know the Truth of who You are.

"Father, have You been anxiously awaiting the time when I am awake?
Time that we can joyfully commune with each other again today?
Time that we can, and shall, spend together?"

"Yes." You softly whisper to my spirit.

Your Voice echoes deep within me;
Spreading Your Profound and Magnificent Love throughout
my entire being.

I feel You so strongly. I breathe You in.
My Father. My Friend. My God; My Everything.
Oh, how I love You!

How can I not love You?
It was You who first overwhelmed me with Your Beautiful
and Radiant Love.

Now my Love for You has its own heartbeat; its own life.

TRIUMPHANT

"Good Morning Father," I say, and joyfully smile.

"Good Morning My beloved one."

You whisper, and Exquisitely Love.

Compassion

*I will be glad
and rejoice in your love,
for you saw my affliction
and knew
the anguish of my soul.*

Psalm 31:7, NIV

TRIUMPHANT

Freedom in Christ is everything. It propels you towards inhabiting a place within Him that is unrestrained and unending. To have your freedom built upon Jesus' foundation is the equivalent of being on eagles wings which takes you farther, deeper, and higher than you could ever have thought possible. Unbound by unnecessary weights, seeing through spiritual eyes, and living for Him allows us this glorious freedom. We can walk through all valleys and fear no evil because He is with us wherever it is that we shall go.

~Marnie~

Freedom

Released, unchained, unlocked; yes me.
Is this what it's like to be set free?

No weights, no worries, no cares, no blocks.
I can dance, I can sing, and out praise the rocks.

Jubilation, exaltation, celebration, galore.
We shall shout and cry out forever more.

I am light, I am floating, and freedom is mine.
I'll be of good use till the end of all time.

Free to hear, to be led, no longer to doubt
what God's Will for my life is truly about.

I'm free - yes I'm free - not bowed in a pit.
Not slave to a thing which desires my quit.

MARNIE BAKER

I'm free and You reign what shall I do now?
Serve in peace, and in Love, of this I do vow.

What's Your Will my True King?
What's Your child now to do?
I'm free, yes indeed
I'm now all brand new.

Widows, orphans, strangers, friends
I will treat them as myself.
Your Words, Your Life, Your Love,
is no longer on the shelf.

I must exalt Your Name my Savior,
You shall be glorified through me.
For what You have done for each of us
all eyes shall forever see.

Lord, I want for You to send me
to him, to her, and them.
To here, to there, and everywhere
for You; to be Your gem.

So that all the earth may witness
Your Glory, Your Light, Your Work;
they shall see this Love is not of me,
and Your commandments I do not shirk.

Freedom You have given me
to declare, decree, proclaim;
that God is Ruler over all,
and all shall know His Name.

Jesus is our Rescuer
indeed He holds the key,
to open all the locks and bolts
that once so long held me.

TRIUMPHANT

I can never do enough for Him,
nor can I go too far.
A prison door once held me tight,
but now I am His star.

A jewel within His Crown,
a name upon His Hand.
In Beauty, in Strength, He came for me
and healed, restored my land.

Freedom is my reward from Him,
and the fruit thereof I eat.
For God has seen me at my worse,
and still He washed my feet.

He washed them with His Love and Life,
and now I'm completely clean.
From my head down to my new found heart,
it's amazing and shall be seen.

Seen in action and seen praising,
seen accomplishing His Will.
He shall forever be my Love and Life
today, and tomorrow still.

Freedom to do, to say, to live, to be,
through me and in accord.
My Hope, my Peace, my untold Joy
is Jesus Christ my LORD.

~Dedicated to Roz ~

Delightful

So be truly glad!
There is a wonderful joy ahead,
even though
the going is rough
for a while down here

1Peter 1:6, TLB

TRIUMPHANT

When the poem *Triumphant* first landed in my spirit it began with a sound; a deep rhythmic, worshipful, and joyously wonderful praise. It was then followed by a series of visual pictures, and as soon as I set pen to paper it became more than I ever imagined.

There are 7 parts to this story poem. My recommendation is that you do not read it in its entirety in one sitting. Take your time, read through a chapter or two at a time, and then reflect on what God is speaking and working within your spirit and your heart.

Triumphant

Part 1

~The End, and The Beginning~

Living your day to day; dreaming your dreams making your way -
    loving,
crying, and laughing, When suddenly….

BOOM!!!!!!!!!!!!!

A tremendous explosion of power and light erupts all around you.
The forceful intensity hits you full on. Its impact stuns you - bone
    deep.

The thunderous blast rips across the universe, enveloping

everything in

its entirety. Suddenly, your spirit awakens on a phenomenal level. It surges fiercely within you, and is totally on fire. Its revival feels as if a multitude of lightning bolts has struck it repeatedly.

The violent shock vibrates through you, and all around you. You
       are
aware that a certainty and a truth are at hand.

You have been summoned.

Dynamic power has been unleashed from Heaven. Intense
       electricity
slams into your core. The sheer authority of it rocks furiously throughout your entire being.

You gasp. Your eyes instantly close in an instinctive blink. Within
       that
timeless blink everything quakes, everything shatters, and
       everything
changes.

You are distinctly aware that the time is here. It has come. The Plan has been fulfilled. Everything is now complete.

Though your eyelids are still frozen within that timeless blink, you immediately sense that you are elsewhere. You are somewhere
       entirely
different from when your eyelids first descended along their downward path a split second ago. Or was it an eternity ago?

The very atmosphere surrounding you has changed. There is now Excellence in the air. It is Blessed. It is Holy. It is True.

Then, you begin to feel it. Something new and more marvelous
       than

TRIUMPHANT

anything you have ever experienced before. Something remarkable and exceptional is touching you. Its overwhelming magnificence takes your breath away, and bliss overtakes you.

It is *LOVE*. Raw, Unfiltered, Pure, and Perfect *LIVING LOVE*.

Love Itself is touching you. Love Itself is washing over you. Love which is Astonishing in Its depth, and Superior in Its Quality. Love which is Impeccable.

Its Intensity and Beauty saturates everything that you are. It is a Profound and Surpassing Love. It over-runs every part of you; leaving nothing untouched, everything embraced – changing you
forever.

Thoroughly, it envelops you. Your spirit is unable to contain Love
such
as this. It is impossible for it to do so. For This Love is far too great, and far too superb.

It is Unconditional Love. It is Extravagant Love. Its source is found here. It abides here. Love Itself completely surrounds you. Love
Itself
moves within and around you. Love Itself wants nothing more
than to
be near you.

Love rejoices that you are here. Love is elated at your arrival. Love greets you delightedly. Love reaches out to you. Love whispers
your
name, shouts your name, and sings your name.
Love Itself sings to your spirit

"You are here!
You are here!
My Precious,
My Beloved,
You are Home!"

You can do nothing but humbly bow; in reverence, in awe, in honor.
For you are in the Presence of The Lord; The Almighty Living God.
The Everlasting LORD. The One Whose Name is **I AM**!

He IS this Living Love; the Love which is surrounding you. The Love
which is pouring Itself upon you. He is the Love which is joyful at your arrival.

Your spirit reaches out to Him. Accepts Him. Holds Him close; deep
within. Exquisite!

Immediately an unequaled fragrance caresses you. Its perfume is fragrant; wonderful. Ideal.

All at once you feel a glorious Light surrounding you. Its warmth and
richness baths you; cocoons you, soothes you. The peace that it brings

TRIUMPHANT

is unimaginable.

You are still within your timeless blink when the glorious Light
penetrates your eyelids. Its radiance is warm; beckoning.

Slowly you open your eyes.

No life experiences, no human understandings, no hopes, no
    dreams,
not even the highest and most limitless of imaginings can prepare
    you
for this.

For no human mind is able to fully comprehend, nor even think
possible anything close to what you are now beholding. Mere
    words
fail to explain it all. For no earthly words have been formed which
    can
describe the sheer exquisiteness of what you are now seeing.

Only emotions can begin to touch it; can ponder its infinite
    splendor, can
capture its essence. You stand enthralled. Speechless. You try your
    best to
absorb the vast depth of the unimaginable and unequalled Majesty.

It goes far beyond all of what you have ever believed possible. The
world has no reference for Beauty such as this. No one can grasp it.
It is beyond all compare.

You are in Heaven.

You have been summoned to the Throne of The Great I AM;
to the side of The Majesty on High.

He speaks to you; **Abba, our Heavenly Father** – and reaching out

to
you, He says *"Welcome Home My love, My heart, My joy. Come, Let us spend all of time together."*

Unspeakable joy engulfs your entire being. Your spirit soars. It
    swells
with Love so overflowing that it staggers you. You take your first
    step
towards Him; The One Who Loves you the most. With each golden
step you become ever more a part of His Story; The Story of all
Eternity- The Love Story which shall last for all time.

TRIUMPHANT

Part 2

~Zion~

There is a magnificent sound coming from the deepest deep of
    Heaven.
It is a poetic, sweet, and glorious song that is exalting and jubilant.
    Its
intensity penetrates your spirit, and its rhythm cascades
    throughout all
of Heaven. Its elegant tune is flawless. It is Beautiful. It is Alive!

This wondrous sound is the blissful song created by innumerable
    spirits
worshipping God as one. Spirits from every tongue, every tribe,
    and
from every nation; each of us called, treasured, and Loved by Him.

In one accord we celebrate Him. Yet, we also dance our own dance,
and sing our own song. Each with our own story, our own
relationship, and our own intimate Love affair with Him.

No instruments are playing; for it is our spirits which are
    circulating
and magnifying the extraordinary and breathtaking symphony of
    our
worship, of our praise, and of our Love.

With all that we have, and with all that we are, we exceedingly
    glorify
Him. For He is worthy. His Love for us flows throughout all of
    Heaven,
space, and time. His Love Song unites with our own.

MARNIE BAKER

His Love Song is Perfect Perfection; full of joy for us, care over us,
and complete Astonishing Love for one, and for all. Our song
> weaves
together superbly with His. Our spirits are tenderly caressed with
> each
note poured from Him; He is our Living Love Song.

Our spirits respond in rapturous bliss. We shout out in sheer
> happiness.
Our dance becomes more spirited, and the freedom we experience
> is
continuously unleashed. Our spirits trumpet Our Saviors Great and
Holy Name.

Jesus!

So nourishing is His Name. It feeds our spirits. His Name more
> than
satisfies the instinctive thirst and hunger rooted deep within us.
> There is
no other Name like it. It quickens our spirits, and soothes our souls.
> It
is the Name which brings endless hope, and an immeasurable
> portion
of Love

Jesus!

So wonderful to speak and to sing it aloud. His Name fuels our
> passions,
defines our purposes, and fulfills our destinies. Just hearing His
> Name
and we naturally exhale out all the insufferable bad, and breathe in
> His
Remarkable Good.

TRIUMPHANT

Goodness as a balm pours over us; draping us in His Infinite Glory, and His Absolute Holiness. We joyfully exclaim His Just and Magnificent Name.

Part 3

~Our Wellspring~

Before time began; before the earth was formed, before we were
    created
by His Will - there was a Love, a Devotion, a Tenderness which
    yearned
to express Himself. The LORD God, our Creator's heartfelt desire,
called us to be and we were. Spoke a Destiny over us, and it
    became.
We are His Perfect Handiwork; His Masterpiece.

Created by Him to be *Loved*, and to *Love;* to be cherished sons and
daughters, intimate friends, and joint heirs alongside His Precious
    Son
Jesus.

We are His outstanding and flawless Bride. We shine impeccably;
as pure, brilliant gold. Being the Source of our everything is Who
    He is -
being there for us is what He does.

Part 4

~The Dawning~

Our arrival was spectacular. Divine! The Word spoke the Word
and His Plan became manifest; God with us. Life everlasting.
Love eternally given.

Creator, and His Creation. A covenant relationship filled with
endless affection, and exceeding care.

Within His Garden of care and provision, blessed beginnings of
    comfort
and peace was ours. Intimate expressions of nurturing and Love
    were
freely and joyously given. Yet, destruction came - subtly disguised.
It lied. It manipulated. It deceived.

Yet, Justice arose. A Promise was made; was boldly declared.
    Salvation
was commanded; Decreed In Authority.

A Profound and Prophetic Hope was sent forth.
A Promise born.
The Word became Flesh.
Flesh became Hope.
Hope became Resurrection.
Resurrection became Salvation.
Salvation became Restoration.
Restoration became Victory.
And Victory became Triumph.

Part 5

~An Anointed Army~

Empowered by Love, an Anointed Army is born. An impactful
  battle
cry came forth from Jesus; filled with Power and Authority it
  pierced
our spirits. *"Take a stand Mighty Warriors! Choose!"*
Responding to His call, answering His charge, and fighting for the
  side
of Love - We chose Him!

Jesus; Justice and Righteousness - Commander of the Army of The
LORD - leads our Divinely orchestrated footsteps. Forever He shall
uphold us with His Powerful Right Hand.

In Him we are purposeful and victorious. Washed in His life
  changing
Blood. Sealed with His Wonderful Name. The Cross emblazoned
  upon
our Mighty warrior chests. On the battlefield we are strategic; we
  take
our assigned positions, swords drawn and poised to strike- hearts
  on
fire for Him - our Commander, and Our King.

Our muscles are quick, forceful, and disciplined by adversity. We
  now
understand that everything we went through, and endured, was
  not in
vain. For our challenges shaped our determination, and made
  strong as
steel our faith.

TRIUMPHANT

Our will is to follow Jesus, the King of All Glory, wherever it is that
He
leads us. For we love Him. He is our Life, and our Hope.
Everything
that we are comes from Him.

Dynamic, unrelenting, and undefeatable we are. Pursuing,
engaging and
destroying the enemy; leaving nothing alive which stands against
LOVE; against God's Masterful Plan.

Moving as one we are fierce, decisive, controlled. A rampaging
army of
God's Glorious Light; formidable soldiers, skilled to destroy,
equipped
to seize, to hold, to conquer, and to *LOVE.*

We are mighty in battle. Impressive, dominant, purposeful, and
sure.
Advancing the Kingdom of God in Power, Strength and Love.

The enemy sought our destruction; our death. Yet, the Word of the
Lord shall not return void, and God's Perfect Plan will be fulfilled.

For on that *LOVE* filled day, when Jesus gave and finished it all, He
spoke to His Father and said, ***"Not My Will, but Yours."***

Jesus leads us to a victorious Truth. One that the enemy still tries to
deny; that our resurrected Lord is truly The Son of God.

And on the battlefield we fight for Him, and with Him. For with
Him
we win not just the many small battles, but the entire and final war.

Part 6

~Fulfillment Achieved~

Timing was everything.

The battles are now over, the war has been won,
and we have finished strong.

From the beginning of all time our victory was assured.
The crowns upon our heads shine brilliantly;
resting there forevermore.

Our celebration is exhilarating, wondrous!
Our outcry is victorious. Its thundering and triumphant roar
    quakes
throughout all of space and time.

We are here with Him; Our Savior, Our God, Our King.
We shout out in Triumph, we shout out in praise.
We shout out His Wonderful, Everlasting Name - Jesus!

Now we rejoice, we celebrate. We have run our race, and did not
    quit.
We suffered and grieved, yet, we persevered. We were attacked
    and
wounded, but we overcame. We prevailed in His Beauty, by His
    Spirit,
and in His Truth. And through it all we were *Loved* by Him.

Here in Heaven we hold His Banner high. Our flags proclaim
our Lord, our King, our Savior; Jesus Christ.

Ribbons of breathtaking colors stream through the air.

TRIUMPHANT

Our victory cry is rapturous. The music of our spirits beat
    throughout
all of Heaven, and we dance with our whole hearts.

In joyous abandonment all of Heaven worships The Holy One;
The *LOVE* which Loves us all.

Praise rings out for the fulfillment of His Perfect Plan;
to unconditionally Love His children, and to united with them
forever and ever and ever.

Part 7

~Time without End~

The Glory of the Everlasting Lord surrounds us, everywhere. It
    moves
between us, stands beside us, and flows within us. His Exquisite
    Caress
quickens our spirits, and drenches us in His Incomparable Love for
    all
time.

He celebrates us; celebrates that we are here with Him - His
    beloved
sons and daughters. The Lord our Shepherd bestows Loving care
    and
exquisite tenderness upon one and all; as if we are priceless - more
precious than the entire abundance of Heaven itself.

His knowledge of you and I is so deeply intimate, so utterly
    Beautiful.
Creator and creation. There is no closer bond; there is no deeper
    accord.

He is Jehovah Shammah; *The Lord Is There*. Therefore, He is more
than enough to spend all of time with you, and also with me. An
    infinity
of adoring and delighting over us. Peace flowing everlastingly from
Him - and our hearts are thoroughly at rest - submersed in
    Perfectly
Lavish Love.

We have won our Great Reward; **HIM**. The crowns on our heads,
the wholeness that we are now experiencing, and the joy which we

TRIUMPHANT

now live in all pale in comparison with spending a mere moment
wrapped in Jesus' Arms.

Yet, we get to spend time without end wrapped in His Arms. And
    in
His Arms we are fulfilled; whole and complete - in all measure.
We are home. Forevermore.

The realization of His Love created us; It walked with us, and
summoned us to live here with The Father-The Great I AM, His
    Son
Jesus-our Wonderful Savior, and The Holy Spirit-our Eternal
Comforter. The Holy Trinity; The Holy One.

From the beginning, and through God's Amazing and Perfect Plan
    we
are Triumphant; Created for Victory, and Destined for Glory.

Inseparable

*For I am convinced that nothing
can ever separate us
from his love.
Death can't, and life can't.
The angels won't,
and all the powers of hell itself
cannot keep God's love away.
Our fears for today,
our worries about tomorrow,
or where we are-
high above the sky,
or in the deepest ocean-
nothing will ever be able to separate us
from the love of God
demonstrated by our Lord Jesus Christ
when he died for us*

Romans 8:38-39, TLB

TRIUMPHANT

I wrote *Stronger* on a particularly painful day in my life. The first line is an old saying that suddenly popped into my head, and I felt led to sit down and allow my heart to have its say in response.

Stronger

What doesn't kill you makes you stronger?
I'm not sure I would agree.
For right now weak, vulnerable, terrified,
is the sum of all of me.

My trial has lasted far too long,
on this you can rely.
And in its wake, at hells true gate,
is a pain that does not die.

They say that love is like a death,
a thing to not be stirred.
But if one's heart has met its match,
what's then therefore deserved?

Too late, much too late, is the truth of it
for the heart demands its own.
For nothing short of its match will do,
the desire intense and strong.

Skin deep, bone deep, cell deep, core
is the path this love does take.

MARNIE BAKER

Is this then closed; a bolted door,
when my heart love does forsake?

All I know, and all I have, is deeper still inside
for God says to me again, once more
"Daughter, your love is not denied."
"It shall be, It shall do, It shall flourish so true -
Take My Rest, Wear My Peace,
Soak in My Love anew."

My Father, My Friend; Great Lord and King,
My Help from up above.
My hope, my faith, my heart grows weak
as I walk, wait, and dream in love.

See my heart, hear my heart, feel my heart my Lord
for I have done as You have said.
Yet, happiness eludes my battered heart
and instead therein is dread.

Wonderful Jesus - Sweet, Sweet Jesus,
please, oh please, remain.
My life, my hope, my destiny
in You is not in vain.

Remember me therefore My King,
remember me I cry
for in You there is only truth,
in You there is no lie.

~Dedicated to Angela & Cheryl~

TRIUMPHANT

Caring

*Let him have all your worries and cares,
for he
is always thinking about you
and
watching everything
that concerns you*

1 Peter 5:7, TLB

"Why do I worry when God is in control?" How many times have you asked yourself that question? We know and understand that God is in control, and that He has our best interest at the center of His Thoughts, yet worry we do. I wrote *Mindful* as a reminder to each of us that God is always mindful of every single thing that concerns us; from the smallest details of our day to the plans that He has lovingly prepared for our lives.

So, with a Living, Loving God who cares for you and me to such a degree the question truly is *"why is it that we worry so much?"* My prayer for each of us is to let go of the worry, and to intentionally increase our faith and trust in Him.

~Marnie~

<u>Mindful</u>

Why do I struggle
    when things look so grim,
when the smallness of me
    and the vastness of Him,
should make it ok
    should make it all well,
yet, fear and weakness
    are the places I dwell?

Does it make me feel better
    in darkness to roam,
when in God there is Light -
    in Him there is Home?

TRIUMPHANT

When will I get it?
　　When shall I grasp?
He is Truth, He is Life
　　He is *ALL* that I ask.

He is mindful of me
　　in every possible way.
By my side, through it all;
　　forever He'll stay.

How can this be?
　　Mindful of me?
　　My every care and woe?
Holy You are,
　　Your Throne so high - yet,
　　You look so far down below.

Through my day to day,
　　my wants and needs;
　　my every heart's desire.
You make me feel
　　more precious than gold,
　　Your Love; there is none higher.

Blessed to have you my Father,
　　my Hope, my Friend;
　　my Help from up above.
Mindful of me?
　　How can this be?
　　By Thee I am forever *LOVED!*

Worthy

From the end of the earth
I will cry to You,
When my heart is overwhelmed;
Lead me to the rock
that is higher than I.

Psalm 61:2, NKJV

God is perfect in all of His Ways, and one of those ways is that He is *Perfect Living Peace*. Therefore, because of Who and What He is, we can securely anchor ourselves in Him and live within His Peace. Unfortunately, there are times when we allow fear, worry, and doubt to rob us of resting our circumstances upon the pillar of His Peace. What can we do to change this? Well, one way is to quiet the negative noise within and around us: our thoughts, false mindsets, and even our words and our actions. How do you daily walk this out? There is an answer in which certain requirements from us are critical.

The main requirement is to keep our focus zeroed in on God. We must also surrender whatever is robbing us of our peace over to Jesus. We must lay it down before Him and leave it there; we must never give ourselves permission to go back and pick it up again - for its cost to do so will be more worries, more doubts, and more fears. Without the worry and fear we will remain steady and unshakable within Him, and have rest for our souls. Through Jesus we can be filled daily with His *Perfect Living Peace* so that we can move forward with our lives blissfully resting in Him.

<u>Peace Is What I need</u>

Dear Peace,

Why are you so elusive to me? Why can't you and I relax, get acquainted, and settle in together? Why are we not like an old,
    happily
married couple; content, comfortable, and committed? Why, when I

believe that I have found you -and I am resting during my storm -
do I
lose my grip on you?

Jesus said to Peter when he faltered while walking upon the water
"You of little faith, why did you doubt?"[1] The wind and the waves
were there before Peter stepped out of the boat, so why did he
falter at
that moment? Was it fear as well? Is my faith so easily swayed by
the zeal of the winds and the size of the waves of my trials?

Jesus said *"Peace I leave with you; my peace I give you. I do not
give to you as the world gives. Do not let your hearts be troubled
and do not be afraid."*[2] It is a promise of peace; gifted to me by
Him,
and mine by right. It is a treasure bestowed - to be owned forever.
It is
a wondrous land to inhabit; a beautiful place to be.

Peace - I must eat you as honey so that you sustain me, and rock
me to
sleep. Peace - you shall purge the fear and worry as I walk upon the
waters. I shall not be moved by the stormy winds and waves of my
many trials. Yes, they remain; the winds do howl, and the waters
crash
upon me, yet I remain calm, wrapped up tightly wearing Jesus'
Peace.

Living Peace walks towards me as He walked towards Peter. He
walks
beside me, behind me, and hovers above me; breathing His Breath
—
His Perfect Sweet Peace upon me.

And yes, with His Word, He can calm my raging storm. Yet, how
beautiful it is when His Wonderful Living Peace calms me instead.

TRIUMPHANT

Sincerely,

A blessed spirit which belongs to God

~Dedicated to Dorothy~

Rejoicing

*I lift up my eyes to the mountains-
where does my help come from?
My help comes from the LORD,
the Maker of heaven and earth.
He will not let your foot slip-
he who watches over you
will not slumber;*

Psalm 121:1-3, NIV

Being a visual person, I first saw *They Thought They Had Me* in my spirit before the words were given to me. What I saw was someone who had been stripped of everything standing in a small prison cell and the door slamming shut. The slamming cell door was meant to crush them, to make them feel as if absolutely everything had been taken away; that they were now emptied, and abandoned.

As Christ followers we are aware of persecutions, of hatred, and of attacks from all around. Our foes believes that stripping us of things that turn to dust will defeat and silence us. Our foes believes that we are weak, helpless, and easily distracted. Our foes believes that we will fold when faced with opposition.

Our foes cannot comprehend or understand that what makes us sing, what fills us with Love, what is our Hope, and our Joy are not found in the things on this Earth. Our Truth, as well as our Life, is found in God; who is in Heaven and within us. *We will never be defeated because our Father is Untouchable, Everlasting, and He will never leave us nor forsake us.*

<u>They Thought They Had Me</u>

Upon this earth -

They can take away from me
    my house.
They can take away from me
    my land.
They can take away from me
    my joy.

They can take away from me
    my health.
They can take away from me
    my strength.
They can take away from me
    my freedom.
They can take away from me
    my dream.
They can take away from me
    my life.
But, upon all the earth,
    and within all of Heaven;

God *IS*
    my House.
God *IS*
    my Land.
God *IS*
    my Joy.
God *IS*
    my Health.
God *IS*
    my Strength.
God *IS*
    my Freedom.
God *IS*
    my Dream.
God *IS*
    my Life.

And they will **NEVER**
    be able
to take Him away from me,
    or me from Him.

Merciful

*he saved us,
not because of righteous things
we had done,
but because of his mercy.
He saved us through the washing
of rebirth
and renewal
by the Holy Spirit*

Titus 3:5, NIV

There are days when life can be more difficult, more stressful, and filled with more heartache and pain. On those days we may not feel like conquerors; we may feel tired, beat up, and just want to lie down and cry. Those days are not unusual for any of us. We are human beings and we hurt when we get hit, and we bleed when we are cut.

I wrote this poem to share that we are all in this together - that everyone has days where they believe that they are not doing their very best; not feeling powerful and strong in Jesus. Although these days are perfectly natural to experience, we should rest in the fact that we have a Conqueror in Jesus Christ whom we can lean on during our darkest and loneliest times.

~Marnie~

Am I Doing My Very Best

Am I doing my very best?
Today, I'd say I'm not.
Usually I'm upbeat and happy
doing the things that I've been taught.

Like warring in the spirit
and praying down strongholds with fire.
But, lately I've been quiet; reserved,
feeling disturbed, and rather tired.

God has established my footing in Him,
and in all the things above.
Gave me His Redemption and His Grace,
His Peace, His Hope, His Love.

TRIUMPHANT

Yet, lately I've quit singing,
not smiling, and stopped laughing.
For my eyes have not yet seen
what my heart has been dearly asking.

Am I doing my very best?
No, I'd say not at all.
For my hope and peace are not there
and good days I can't recall.

I'm walking through the motions,
not going deep - it's true.
How can I shake this doom and gloom?
I truly wish I knew.

I know God's Word, I know His Power,
I know His Wonders, and His Love.
But what I don't know is why no answers,
why no breakthrough from Heaven above.

I do not belong in a pit;
in darkness or despair.
I need Your help Almighty One
to know Your Truly there.

To guide me through the darkest nights,
to help me through the fields;
of mines, and traps, and tricky snares,
Please bring Your Mighty Shield.

I need the sea to part for me,
I need the sun to shine.
I need Your Love to conquer all,
and make it all just fine.

I'm exhausted, weak, and failing,
and hope - I can no longer abide.
For it sets me up to believe in something
which is continuously denied.

"Have faith dear child, have faith so true,
for you are not alone.
My Son has accomplished all for you
when MY POWER rolled away that stone.

His Death and Resurrection
was not so you would cry.
It was set in motion to tell the Truth;
Now in Him be healed; revived.

Take that tissue and dry your eyes,
and see with Mine your worth.
For I have given ALL of dearest price,
and am LORD and KING on earth.

So that you may know I AM The LORD,
and beside Me there is none.
I shall take away the pain and hurt,
and send to you my Son.

Open your heart to receive My Gift,
and allow it to be healed.
My Word will accomplish all you need;
My Son is your hearts Great Shield.

The LORD shall heal and care for you,
I am willing and able to decree;
to destroy the mountains,
answer your doubts,
and to part your raging seas."

TRIUMPHANT

Am I doing my very best?
He's within me and that's all I need.
I can ask for help, and He rescues me-
with Jesus, I shall succeed.

Destiny

*Many are the plans
in a person's heart,
but it is the LORD's purpose
that prevails.*

Proverbs 19; 21, NIV

TRIUMPHANT

God is Perfect in every way and when He enters into your heart, and your life, there are immense benefits and blessings that come along with Him. I wrote this poem because I know that *With Him* there is no better life that I could possibly have. There is nothing that could sway me away from God, for with Him I am everything that I am meant to be.

With Him

With Him I am

Loved upon Loved upon Loved
Saved upon Saved upon Saved
Blessed upon Blessed upon Blessed
Shielded upon Shielded upon Shielded
Treasured upon Treasured upon Treasured
Rejoicing upon Rejoicing upon Rejoicing

With Him there is

Hope upon Hope upon Hope
Peace upon Peace upon Peace
Joy upon Joy upon Joy
Care upon Care upon Care
Trust upon Trust upon Trust
Glory upon Glory upon Glory

MARNIE BAKER

With Him I have

Truth upon Truth upon Truth
Faith upon Faith upon Faith
Provision upon Provision upon Provision
Possibilities upon Possibilities upon Possibilities
Reward upon Reward upon Reward
Dream upon Dream upon Dream

With Him He gives

Grace upon Grace upon Grace
Mercy upon Mercy upon Mercy
Promise upon Promise upon Promise
Healing upon Healing upon Healing
Goodness upon Goodness upon Goodness
Freedom upon Freedom upon Freedom

With Him

Everything
Great, and Pure,
Perfect, and Wonderful,
Compassionate, and Loving is found.

Beautiful

Because the Lord
is
my Shepherd,
I have everything
I need!

Psalm 23:1, TLB

After accepting and receiving God into our hearts we each go through many life changing transformations. These transformations change us for the better; into the new creation that we are becoming through Christ Jesus. With our new birth in Him we are able to embrace the brand new heart that He has created for us. This transformed heart allows us to step into the new life that He has prepared for us. I wrote *New Clothes* to represent our Divine transformation with Jesus.

~Marnie~

New Clothes

Old heart, old mind, old past,
old friends, old choices, old burdens,
old cares, old behaviors, old sins
old me.

New heart, new mind, new life,
new friends, new choices, new blessings,
new character, new beginnings, new gifts
new destiny.

Old patterns, old curses, old pits,
old deceptions, old thoughts, old limits,
old pains, old fears, old baggage
old struggles.

New joys, new freedoms, new hopes,
new Love, new family, new future,

TRIUMPHANT

new happiness, new peace, new joys
new birth.

Not perfect… Yet, clean new clothes.

Gracious

"Bring my soul out of prison {adversity},
So that I may give
thanks and praise Your name;
The righteous
will surround me {in triumph},
For You
will look after me."

Psalm 142:7, AMP

I wrote *Better, Stronger, Faster, Greater* because when I think about who I am, and what I am all about, I can never separate any part of myself from God. I am, in all totality, ALL God's. He is the sum of me; every breath, every portion, and every atom. I can truly say that I am His, and He is mine.

Better, Stronger, Faster, Greater

The sum of me -
    with all of its intricate pieces and parts:

My surpassing accomplishments,
    and my painful failures.
My highest of hopes,
    and my dreamiest of dreams.
My hearts desires,
    and my deepest emotions.
My particular habits,
    and my personal limitations.
My funny little quirks,
    and my delightful eccentricities.
My abilities long and short,
    and my qualities great and small.

~And even more~

My present and future goals,

and my aspirations - high and low.
My leaping successes,
    and my bitterest of disappointments.
My name,
    where I came from,
    and where I am going.

~And deeper still~

My experiences;
    good and bad.
My highs;
    earthly and Heavenly.
My lows;
    deep and many.

    ~And so~
From the length of each and every strand of my hair,
    down to the very tips of my fingernails -
    every single nook and cranny of me
    belongs to, and is, God's!

Not because we are Creator and creation,
    or that I am His beloved child;
    It is because I have chosen Him.

I Have Chosen God!

I have breathed Him in
    and declared Him as my entire being.
I have given over the sum of me;
    absolutely and completely.

My choice has not made my life worry
    or stress free.
It has not made it without pain or grief
    yet, I could not take a safe

TRIUMPHANT

or redemptive step without Him.

Good days or bad,
    Understanding it all or not -
    I choose God.

With Him; I am better, stronger, faster,
    and greater
    than I ever dared dreamed was possible.

Love

*We love Him
because
He first loved us.*

1John 4:19 NKJV

TRIUMPHANT

Jesus is not only our Savior and our Redeemer - our Light and Love - He is also a Righteous, Mighty, Warrior. He Faithfully and Justly commands the victorious – *The Triumphant* - Army of the Lord. We are in the spiritual army of King Jesus, and we serve the only One Who is Worthy, Honorable, and True.

My Commander

When arrows come
    and come they will,
His strength in me
    will not sit still.

As storms brew up
    with wind and rain,
I shall not bow down
    or kneel to pain.

When mountains arise
    and shutter and shake,
God's True Word
    will calm its quake.

For Jesus is Lord
    from beginning to end.
He comforts and guides;
    He's truly our Friend.

MARNIE BAKER

For He is not weak
    or caught unaware,
He knows that I need Him
    before beginning my prayer.

My shield is His Love
    my weapon - His Word,
my shelter - His Care
    in Him I will gird.

I am empowered and able
    to war and to win.
For Jesus is Commander
of the army I'm in.

For truth, and for justice;
    for what's right, and not wrong,
He has called me by name
    and now I'm quite strong.

On the battlefield I'm disciplined
    and sharp as a blade.
Precise and relentless,
    no mercy - not swayed.

My foe is quite subtle
    yet his tricks are not new.
His tactics are obvious,
    and lies he does spew.

A warrior, a conqueror,
    victorious - all power.
I slay for God's Kingdom;
    I don't yield, nor cower.

I destroy absolutely,
    I strike until dead.

TRIUMPHANT

My foe, it is lifeless,
    then I take its foul head.

I am quite undefeatable,
    and engaged till the end.
As long as I fight
    my will does not bend.

Ruthless and powerful,
    steady and sure,
a merciless weapon
    the battlefield secure.

My Commander is here also,
    and I'm under His Wing.
Yes! I know Who I fight for;
Jesus! Lord, and Great King!

promises

*and be sure of this-
that I am with you always,
even to the end of the world."*

Matthew 28:20, TLB

TRIUMPHANT

Early one morning, during my prayer time, I kept repeating the first line of *Comforter* over and over again. I knew then that I had to sit down and allow my heart to write down what it longed to say to God. Here is my hearts voice as it *Lovingly* worships our Amazing and Magnificent Heavenly Father.

Comforter

To the One who is my Comforter,
The One who Loves me so;
The One who breathes such hope in me,
with Him I shall always know

That I am highly favored,
beyond all I comprehend.
For He is my very heart and soul;
my Love, my Life, my Friend.

To the One Who is my Comforter
from Whom True Love does flow,
I gift to You my heart, my life
On a platter - they are bestowed.

To be swaddled in pure Love as His
is to know bliss beyond compare.
For I'm deeply and truly adored by Him;
I'm His child, His joy, His heir.

Faithful

I love the LORD,
because he has heard my voice
and
my pleas for mercy.
Because
he inclined his ear to me,
therefore
I will call on him
as long as I live.

Psalm 116:1-2, ESV

One of the many things that I love about our Heavenly Father is His openness in sharing with me exactly who I am to Him. The incredible way that He treats me - because of His great and everlasting love for me - blesses me tremendously. I fully embrace my position as His daughter, His treasure, and His beloved. I wrote *I Am His* so that each of us would completely and truly embrace what we mean to God.

It is an undeniable fact that you and I are exquisitely and adoringly cherished and loved by God. This poem came straight from my heart and my spirit, and my prayer is that all of God's children will walk in the Unfailing Truth of who we are to Him.

<u>I Am His</u>

To be someone who is greater than
my earthly thoughts of me.
Abandon lies, embrace instead
God's Plans that are meant to be.

God says *"I have redeemed you,*
you are a child of Mine.
Step away from that which keeps you
from coming to My Vine."

He says that I am worthy
of all He has said and done.
The fact of this must be true
for He has sacrificed His Son.

MARNIE BAKER

He says that He has called me
by name and I am His.
He yearns to hold me close to Him
so Kind, so Pure, He is.

To know that I am His indeed
to believe in what He says.
To lay aside and depart from lies
which abound within my head.

God looks with Eyes that see me;
my soul, my mind, my thoughts.
He gave what was most dear to Him;
Christ Jesus - my soul He bought.

He says *"You are Mine forever."*
Beloved - He declares that I am.
Nestled, cradled, and treasured; adored
by a Shepherd who *LOVES* His lambs.

Truly You are My Joy, My love,
the one that I sing of and Who,
the One I proclaim - in Your Hand is my name -
declaring a *LOVE* that is true.

Believe Him I shall when He says that I am
lovely, wonderful, and kind.
Inside and out - precious – no doubt,
in Jesus I am sealed, I am signed.

Joyful

*for your love and kindness
are better to me
than life itself.
How I praise you!*

Psalm 63:3, TLB

Early one morning, while I was sitting at my desk, the first line of *Mine* leaped into my spirit. Countless times I have prayed for my heart not to fail me as I wait on the promise that the Lord has given me to come to pass. I speak this poem over each one of us who are waiting, in hope and faith, upon our Wonderful and Faithful Lord.

Mine

Mine is the heart that shall never fail,
to Love, to hope, to dream, to scale.

Scaling cloud brushed mountain tops,
dreaming dreams that shall come true.

Thriving in hope eternally given,
breathing in a life destined only for me.

Surpassing my own limits
because God is without them.

Rejoicing in freedom purchased with Blood
by a timeless Love which beats within.

A heart given to One deserving of its entirety;
worthy of every chamber is He.

My life is overflowing with an outstanding Love;
a universe it does indeed fill.

TRIUMPHANT

Therefore, no longer being my own,
yet, every part of it is *ALL HIS,*

Mine is the heart that
SHALL never fail!

Hallelujah

*"Fear not,
for I have redeemed you;
I have called you by your name;
You are Mine."*

Isaiah 43:1, NKJV

TRIUMPHANT

I wrote the poem *Up* for all those who have been knocked down and who have made the choice not to remain there. It is also for those who have remained there, and need the encouragement to get back up. I witnessed a perfect example of not remaining down with a dear friend who was going through a trial. He chose to keep fighting, even when the answers were not all there, and even when he did not understand it all.

~Marnie~

Up

I have been hit,
    and I am bleeding.

I have been knocked down,
    and I am crying.

I am hurting,
    and feeling the pain.

I have questions,
    and they remain unanswered.

But

There is no way
    that I am staying down.

Not by any means.

MARNIE BAKER

For this is not my story.
  This is not my song.

I am not meant to be here;
    lying on the ground,
    in a cell, or a pit;
    in hopeless despair.

Trials will come and go,
  But, I will not quit.

So, my spirit shouts;

"Wake up!"
  I shall wake up

"Stand up!"
  I shall stand up

"Never give up!"
  I shall never give up

"For Jesus Christ IS Lord!"

    "Hallelujah!"
    " Hallelujah!"
    "Hallelujah!"

~Dedicated to Bill~

peaceful

*"I am leaving you with a gift-
peace of mind and heart!
And the peace I give
isn't fragile like the peace
the world gives.
So
don't be troubled or afraid"*

John 14:27, TLB

When I was living my life without God, I unconsciously believed a lie that was blinding me to the truth. I believed that I could live my life without Him and that it would be ok. No, it was not ok. It was, and is, a lie that has and continues to deceive countless people. Today, I thank God with all of my heart that He never gave up on me. He sent His Son Jesus to relentlessly pursue me with His sustaining and heart mending Love.

Good, Better, Best

Life was good,
then I stumbled.

Life got better,
then it crumbled.

God *SAVED* me
and the rest
remains…

the *BEST*.

Wonderful

*Your beauty and love
chase after me
every day of my life.
I'm back home
in the house of GOD
for the rest of my life.*

Psalm 23:6, MSG

When the appointed day of my salvation arrived, God came to me and became the God of my heart and my life. *I Am Home* is especially close to my heart. I wrote it to share how thankful I am to God for hearing my hearts desperate cry for help that life changing day. Through His Wonderful Grace and Love - God pursued me, wooed me, and rescued me from despair. *I Am Home* celebrates my salvation within His Wondrous and Unending Love. It is written as if there is a conversation taking place between two people; as one person shares with the other their story of salvation and restoration with God.

I Am Home

No longer shall I roam just anywhere;
near or far, here or there.
Nowhere.

{What was life like for you?}

Unsafe, unprotected – fooling myself.
Thinking all is well, life is good,
that I am fine.

{What were you doing?}

Cutting myself off from Love which *Loves* me;
which was calling to me,
which was yearning for me so fiercely.

TRIUMPHANT

{Were you happy?}

I was thirsting and did not know it.
I was hungry and tried almost everything;
yet, tasting nothing.

{God NEVER gives up on us!}

How could I think that I could do without Him?
What kept me away far too long?

{Those are crucial questions}

What was I so afraid of?
My life changing?
My heart being corrected?

{You were running away?}

I was running so hard, and getting nowhere.
Like a top spinning around, and around,
and around.

{Without Purpose}

Hollow inside.
Surrounding myself with counterfeits.
Stumbling around,
yet, believing that I was heading somewhere.

{Truth shall prevail}

Was I afraid to admit that I was never in control?
I knew that everything could be gone suddenly,
yet, I believed.

MARNIE BAKER

{You believed in God?}

I believed in me, myself, and I.
The unbeatable, unstoppable team of me;
Bulletproof, daring, courageous, awesome me.

{His Light and Love will always reveal lies}

I was none of those things.
Just a superficial, skin deep imitation at work.

{How did you live with it?}

I hoped that it would all turn out fine.
That I would not have to commit; to change.

{God was always there for you.}

Then one day I was honest and stopped running.
Everything I had was built on sand.
It would fail.

{Why did you respond to Him at that time?}

The time for running away and believing lies
was over. I craved something more.
Something…necessary.
I needed truth.

{You heard His Call?}

Finally listening, my heart received the Truth.
It settled peacefully upon the foundation of God.

TRIUMPHANT

{You Win!}

Myself has connected to Himself.
No more wandering. No more roaming.
The Love of a Lifetime has *kissed* and *embraced* me.

{God celebrates!}

Yes! Kissed me on both cheeks and invited
all of His friends to rejoice with Him. He wants
them to know that I am where I belong;
that I am His Forever, and that He is mine Forever.

{He IS our Blessed Redeemer!}

Thank you Father for saving me,
receiving me, and for welcoming me.

I am home!

Glorious

My flesh and my heart may fail;
But God is the strength of my heart
and
my portion forever.

Psalm 73:26, NKJV

As God's children we desire to do what is right, to overcome wrong, and to walk in His Righteousness. Still, we are flesh and blood creatures; flawed, weak, and prone to disobedience. I wrote *Redeemed* to demonstrate how our bodies and our minds are often at war with our spirits. In all this, God is our strength when we are weak, and He is our Saving Grace in the times when we need Him the most.

<u>Redeemed</u>

Born to be loved,
yet, why so much pain?

A heart created to feel, to desire, to soar
yet, also impure… treacherous - deceitful.

A mind crafted to expand, to explore, to imagine
yet, also wicked…vain - rebellious.

Which part shall rule me?
Which part shall prevail?

"You are Redeemed!" is God's reply,
is His Heavenly Decree.

"You are worthy of all of Me;
of My Peace and My Victory.
I hold all of you tightly in My Mighty Hand.

MARNIE BAKER

You and I, We shall prevail,
and together, We SHALL stand!"

Victorious

*Truly he is my rock and my salvation;
he is my fortress,
I will never
be shaken.*

Psalm 62:2, NIV

As we face the storms of life we will have to fight; to battle. Many of us do not like to think of ourselves as soldiers, yet spiritual soldiers we are. *Warriors Goal* was written to share that the battle is not ours, but the Lords. We should remove the word 'quit' from our minds because God has given us the weapons necessary to fight from a position of Triumph -for our victory through Jesus is assured.

We should rely on His Strength, His Power, and His Authority and not our own. Let us declare His Victory; let us stand strong, let us believe eternally, and let us always remember who we are with God by our side.

~Marnie~

Warriors Goal

Boundless, dominant strength;
hurdling tall, jagged mountains.
Swimming treacherous, raging rivers.
Sprinting like a gazelle.
Invincible.
Yes, true!

Enemies abound; poisonous and snarling.
Lying in wait, trying to destroy me.
Whispering lies, doubts, and hopelessness.
Darkness surrounds me, clouding my vision.
Distractions. Destruction. Pain.

But I am a Warrior!

TRIUMPHANT

Warrior; Defeater of false lions.
Infinite, dynamic power.
Unstoppable might in action.

Warriors Goal; To Advance The Kingdom of God.

Courage? Fearlessness?
No.
ALL GOD!

He empowers me - qualifies me to be;
Unconquerable flint, Undefeatable weapon,
Child of The Most High God.

Victory was, is, and always shall be
MINE!

Trusting

*For I cried to him
and
he answered me!
He freed me
from all my fears.*

Psalm 34:4, TLB

TRIUMPHANT

Having God in my life is the Greatest Reward that I could ever ask for or desire. He is my Everything. I wrote *I Need Him* to share my Love and my constant want and need for God. I celebrate, praise and worship Him as my Father, my Best Friend, and my Greatest Love.

~Marnie~

I Need Him

I need God - more than I can ever fully say,
for words cannot truly express that my inner being feels
as if it has a Star burning, beating, shining, deep
within the core of me.

A glowing Star that is vibrant and alive;
so wondrous, so empowering.
This hot, radiant Star of Light casts off such beauty,
such peace, and such devastating Love;
The Essence of Pure and True Love Itself.

Dynamic, powerful, and alive;
pulsating with unfathomable Goodness.
To have it centered in my core –
blessed beyond all measure am I.
To know such a thing of Greatness,
to be led by the Epitome of Exquisite Perfection.

Beautiful, Lovely, Wondrous God.
Who or what can ever come close

to you? You bring such Peace.
You bring unspeakable joy.
My spirit leaps at the very thought of You;
of Who You truly are.

Bowing down we all shall cry Holy!
Holy is Who You are.
Holy is What You are.

I cry out and speak to the One I need the most.
Always take me with You; my Love and my King!
The One who is like a Living Star inside of me,
a Guiding Light; a Source of Hope, Faith and Love.
The One Who makes me feel so blessed, so happy, and so alive -
as if I have won a Gift incomparable to any other thing.

I do know that not all my days will seem good.
I do not always understand what life brings my way, or why.
Yet, I do not ever want nor shall I ever live my life without The
One I need the most; Our Magnificent God, and Friend;
The Star within my chest.

Adored

*We know how much God loves us
because we have felt his love
and
because we believe him
when he tells us that he loves us dearly.
God is love,
and anyone who lives in love
is living with God
and God
is living in him.*

1 John 4:16, TLB

Our Day is the result of a glorious day that Jesus and I spent together. It was fun to get to know more about Him in such a relaxed and happy way. I put no needs or requests before Him, as I only wanted to be with Him in communion - just Him and me, smiling into each other's eyes. It was a refreshing day in which we were able to continue to build upon the friendship that He so freely offers to each of us.

Our Day

The sun is shining today;
in the sky, and inside of me.

Smiles surround me; my face is smiling,
my heart is smiling, and my Love is smiling.

Jesus is beaming His Joy down upon me.
I feel it; all around, and within me.
How beautiful it is!
Such Perfection.

I am so happy.
I am so well.
My soul is singing, and my spirit is fed.

Lightness is in my steps.
Laughter is within my words.
My hand is being held by God.

TRIUMPHANT

His Sweet Kisses brush lovingly
across my forehead.

What a Gift He is to me.
Thank you Lord for always being here for me.
Whether I feel You or not
You are never far away.

I know it more today than I did yesterday;
and I will know it even more tomorrow.
There are days like today when I long to be Home
with You even more than usual.
How wonderful it is that you do not wait until
Heaven to Love on me, to spend time with me,
And to make me smile.

Happiness. You are Extravagant Happiness.
You fill me with what so many are missing;
Your Love.

Love. Utter Love. Blessed Love.
Splendid Love. Dynamic Love.

Continue to hold me Wonderful Jesus,
continue to be my Friend.

My heart speaks to You and says …
*"My Great Love, would You like to do
something fun together today?"*

Happily You whisper Your favorite game
to my spirit.

"Yes, let's do that." I say. *"Let's have some fun."*

You smile and shine your heart down upon me,

and Our Day together begins
and becomes even better.

Blessings

*The thief comes only in order
to steal and kill and destroy.
I came
that they may have
and enjoy life,
and have it in abundance
{to the full, till it overflows}.*

John 10:10, AMP

There are times in our lives when things do not always turn out the way that we want them to. Dreams can be unfulfilled, prayers seem to go unanswered, hopes become dashed, or we could lose someone suddenly and unexpectedly.

No matter how much we desire something, or love someone, God is the most important and the most valuable Something and Someone that you could ever have.

Things in our lives come and go, and people are with us for a season; no one and nothing is here forever. God is the Source of ALL and can establish and bring forth more Love, more dreams, and more hopes through Him. Let us hold firmly the fact that the Only True, Everlasting Treasure, and Blessing that we have was, is, and always shall be God.

Gaining Everything

Blindsided. Disappointed.
Confused. Doubtful.
Wavering.

I have no strength left in me. It's much easier to lie here and cry.
Painful, dark, hopeless; a bleak place to be.
So what do I do now?

I have a decision to make: lie here and cry; die here?
Or rise up and move; live on?

Which path will I choose? Which report will I heed?

TRIUMPHANT

Which plans will I instill? Which voice do I silence?

That Eternal Place of Comfort and Peace beckons me.
There is an abundance of Love waiting for me.
I must go; I must be there.

My spirit humbly arrives at God's Gracious Throne.
Just being in His Wonderful Presence strengthens me,
comforts me, and brings sweet rest to my frantic soul.

Once near Him my decision is so beautifully clear.
It was made even before I was formed.
His Path I will walk, His report I will heed,
His Plans for me I will embrace,
and all other voices I will silence.

For He is the only One that is Eternally True;
The One that works continuously for my good.
The One that shall see me through - because He Loves me.

To the Great and Almighty King;
The King who Rules and Reigns forever,
The King Who sits upon a Holy and Everlasting Throne –
I give to You my heartbreaks, my disappointments,
and my unanswered questions.

I tenderly lay down my need to understand.
I place it all at the Feet of the One that I worship and adore.

I bow down to the God of my life and say *"Not my will, but Yours
my King. For the truth is, what if I gained everything that I wanted,
everything that I hoped for, and I lost You My Lord?*

*I would have absolutely NOTHING. My gain would be as meaningless
as pouring sand into a pail with no bottom. However, what if everything
was*

MARNIE BAKER

lost to me? What if it all fell and crumbled into the sea?

What if seeing the fulfillment of the promise, or receiving the desires of my
*   heart,*
was not mine to touch, to feel, to have and yet, I still had You?

Then I would have everything that I could ever need, want, or hope for.
My joy would be unending. For You are the Love, the Need,
the Want, and the Greatest Desire of my entire life."

So, I wrap it all up in a gift box; all of my hopes, my dreams,
and the unfulfilled promises. Kneeling before You,
I place it in Your Hand and say *"Jesus, do as You will with them."*

Releasing, and leaving it with Him; the chains are loosed,
the weight is gone - Freedom arrives.

Smiling joyfully, I raise my hand in Triumph, for I have won.
I have passed the test; I have not forsaken, nor abandoned,
My God for any reason.

With His Grace and His Love I will deal with the pain, the loss,
and the grief - for He shall see me through.

Here I stand - joyful and *Triumphant*. Joyful because I am His,
and I am free.
Triumphant because I have battled and came through,
always and forever, cleaved to His Throne.

I am not Triumphant because I am fearless
and came out unharmed - indeed not.

For I was wounded, and I bled. I trembled, stumbled, and I fell.
I did not always understand it all. I asked God countless *"why's?"*
which were mostly left unanswered.

TRIUMPHANT

You see, I am Triumphant because I remained loyal to the
King of all Kings, no matter what. I remained true and firmly
  believed
in who He knows that I am, and who He has created me to be.

Living in the realization of who you are to Him; this is why you
  win.
This is what makes you Triumphant!

precious

for you have been chosen by God himself-
you are priests of the King,
you are holy and pure,
you are God's very own-
all this
so that you may show to others
how God called you out of the darkness
into his wonderful light.

1 Peter 2:9, TLB

TRIUMPHANT

We each realize that as we go about our lives we will have good days and not so good days. Situations, big and small, will come across our paths which will challenge us. To these challenges we will respond either positively, neutrally, or negatively.

I wrote *There's Always A Choice* to encourage each of us so that whenever we face challenges, prayerfully, our choice of reactions will be positive and sincere through Christ Jesus. By making a positive Christ centered choice, it makes a demand on Christ within us so that we can do better than what we could possibly do on our own.

~Marnie~

There's Always A Choice

Really?
    A choice?
    For you? For me?
    A choice to be, to do, to see?

Why stay down
    when up is better?
Why limp along
    when you were made to run?

Still cool waters,
    God leads me beside.
He stands strong;
    a Tower of Hope and Love.
Breath of Life

MARNIE BAKER

established inside of me,

His Breath;
   So Good, so Wonderful.
   silencing the fears
   so Truth can come in.

Truth;
   No matter what my storm is
   True Love does indeed conquer.
   Always.

True Love:
   It reaches for the stars. It sprouts from far below.
   It Triumphs over death. It cannot be defeated.
   For True Love is God.

True Love climbs invisible walls
   to come for you.
True Love has wings
   and soars high to find you.

True Love
   fights for you.
True Love
   empowers you to stand strong - with Him.

True Love
   is your Friend when death knocks at your door.
True Love
   has your back when the darkness comes.
True Love
   is your partner in everything that you do.

Because True Love exists
   there is always a choice.

TRIUMPHANT

True Love is Alive;
 reaching, and growing.
For True Love is Hope;
 Living, and Strong.
True Love is True;
 incorruptible, and everlasting.

True Love lives because God lives,
 and because God lives
 there is always a choice.

Our circumstances do not
 dictate our responses;
 we do-we choose.

Our emotions are powerful,
 but we have dominion.
Our pain is real,
 but we have a Savior;
 a Help, and a Hope.

For that reason,
 there is a choice available,
 and not choosing is still a choice.

There is despair,
 but you can choose happiness.
There is anger,
 but you can choose peace.
There is offense,
 but you can choose forgiveness.
There is wrong,
 but you can choose right.
There is hate,
 but you can choose love.

For you see…
>Light overcomes darkness.
>Love conquers hate.
Truth does indeed prevail,
>and justice will have its say.

And our greatest choice of all?
>God.

Will it be Him;
>The Light Bringer,
>The Burden Lifter,
>The Key Holder,
>The Soul Soother?

Will it be His Truth,
>His Way,
>and His Love?

Or something else?

We are for a moment.
He is for *ALL* time.

Choose well.

Afterward

If you would like to make Jesus Christ your Lord and personal Savior please read this Salvation Prayer, and receive Him into your heart and life.

<u>Salvation Prayer</u>

Dear Jesus,

I need You Lord. I admit that I am a sinner and I ask for You to forgive me. I believe in my heart, and I confess with my mouth, that You are the Son of God. I believe that You died on the cross for my sins, rose again, and now live forevermore. I accept You as my Lord and Savior, and I receive Your free gift of Salvation and Eternal Life. Please become the God of my heart and life - of which I freely give to You. Jesus, I ask You to lead and guide me through each and every day from this moment on.

Thank You Jesus!

Amen!

Personal Message from Marnie:

What an incredible experience this has been for me. I would like to thank you for joining me on this journey with, and for, God. If Triumphant has been a blessing to you would you go out to Amazon and leave a review? Also, I would love to hear from you - if you have been blessed, or have prayed the Salvation Prayer, please come share your thoughts and your stories with me at:

Triumphant Facebook page: Triumphant; Created For Victory, Destined For Glory

My blog: marnieinlove.com
Email: marnie@marnieinlove.com
Twitter: @marnieinlove
Instagram: marnieinlove

~Marnie~

Endnotes

13 - Peace Is What I need

[1] Matthew 14:31, NIV

[2] John 14:27, NIV

Made in the USA
Charleston, SC
20 April 2016